BILL CASKEY

THE 9 STRATEGIES

HOW TO MODERNIZE YOUR SALES APPROACH TO
RADICALLY GROW YOUR INCOME IN B2B SELLING

Copyright © 2024 by Bill Caskey

All rights reserved. No part of this publication may be reproduced, stored or transmitted in any form or by any means, electronic, mechanical, photocopying, recording, scanning, or otherwise without written permission from the publisher. It is illegal to copy this book, post it to a website, or distribute it by any other means without permission.

Bill Caskey has no responsibility for the persistence or accuracy of URLs for external or third-party Internet Websites referred to in this publication and does not guarantee that any content on such Websites is, or will remain, accurate or appropriate.

If you would like to interview Bill Caskey on your podcast, please reach out to Bill at bcaskey@caskeytraining.com.

To purchase books in large quantities (>25), send request to info@caskeytraining.com.

First edition

DEDICATION

I dedicate this book to all sales professionals, sales leaders, and business owners who are committed to growing their business by growing their skills.

I also dedicate the writing of this to my wife Jane, my daughters, Kelly and Kara, and my current roster of grandchildren, Evan, Sawyer, and Palmer. It's unlikely you'll listen to my 3000 podcasts, but maybe you'll pick up a copy of this book after I'm long gone :-)

CONTENTS

Foreword 1

1. Be More Concerned With Their Outcomes - Not Yours ... 5

2. Get Your Mind Right 9

3. Become Detached From All Outcomes 13

4. Create a Written Strategy 17

5. Get Clear On Your True Assets 22

6. Control The Buyer/Seller Dance 26

7. Rely On Systems - Not Goals 30

8. Sell The Way People Buy 34

9. Take Control Early 39

Conclusion 43

What's Next? 45

FOREWORD

It wasn't meant to unfold this way.
Yet there I was, a 29-year-old surrounded by people who looked like they were on death's doorstep – missing teeth, vacant stares, lives in disarray.

I found myself confined within the stark walls of an alcohol rehabilitation hospital, a place I never imagined I'd end up.

What led me to this point? How did I, someone who 'seemed' to have it all together, end up here?

The truth was, I knew exactly why I was there. **I drank too much.** I was a drunk – fully functioning on the surface, but a drunk nonetheless. And no, I did not have it all together.

As I surveyed my new companions, I realized the grim path that lay ahead if I didn't get my affairs in order — if I didn't stop poisoning myself with alcohol.

You've likely heard similar stories from celebrities and performers who ended up in rehab, claiming they didn't know how they got there. But for me, the reasons were clear – I was trying to medicate some pain from my younger years, a pain that I still can't quite pinpoint to this day.

My upbringing was average, my parents loving, my neighborhood solidly middle-class. I excelled in school, basketball, and other activities.

So what went wrong? Not sure.

I don't dwell on that question anymore. What I do know is that God had a plan for me — one that included hitting rock bottom at Fairbanks Hospital in 1989. Was that **my** plan? Nope. But it was His.

Regardless of your religious beliefs, I believe in the Holy Spirit, and I believe that Divine intervention led me to that pivotal moment. Because without hitting that lowest point, I would not be doing what I'm doing today – coaching sales professionals and business owners to live better versions of themselves.

The fact is that our stories shape us. Whether they are stories of climbing mountaintops or hiding in valleys, who we have been helps us to be who we are today.

My Work

Over the last 30 + years, I've been working with leaders of all kinds, helping them to redefine what it means to be successful. You see, I don't think success is all about numbers of hours worked or dollars in your bank account.

I think success is about personal expression and fulfillment.

I know too many people who make a lot of money who are not fully expressed and certainly not fulfilled. Henry David Thoreau said it perfectly, *"Most men live lives of quiet desperation and die with the song still in their heart."*

I know this may not sound like sales training, but I don't want you to die with a song still in your heart.

So, the purpose of this book is to give you some strategies that I find are missing in most B2B salespeople — and that by deploying them, you will have more clarity and confidence to achieve better outcomes.

You might look at some of these and feel like they are beneath you, but I'd bet if I heard you on the phone talking to prospects and customers, some of these things would be lacking.

My Promise

I'll make the simple promise: If you read and implement these nine strategies in all of your business affairs — whether you're in sales, leadership, or any other business role — I promise you will be more effective in communicating your value to other human beings.

The Format

The format I've chosen to use in this book is:

a. the **strategy** that I believe you should deploy
b. **suggestions** on how to deploy the first step of that strategy
c. and **how it will help you**, where I reinforce several ideas that will inspire you to make this happen.

Without inspiration, change is difficult. I appreciate you joining me on this journey. There are millions of books out there you could have purchased, so I'm grateful to you for choosing mine - and I aim to make this one as important as any you've bought before.

Tell Me Your Story

I love hearing from readers. Email me at info@caskeytraining.com with your story of how you've used these nine strategies to grow your income.

STRATEGY 1

BE MORE CONCERNED WITH THEIR OUTCOMES - NOT YOURS

"The art of conversation lies in listening."
- Malcolm Forbes

This mistake happens because sales managers spend an inordinate amount of time training on features and benefits. And even more time talking about goals, forecasts, revenue cycles, marketing campaigns, etc. It's all about <u>US</u>.

That's not a bad thing, but it misses a key ingredient: **the prospect's problem - that they are willing to spend money and time to fix.**

The fact is, when you get into the sales process, your needs don't matter — at all.

The only thing that matters is you being present in the conversation so that you can determine whether your customer has a problem you can solve or a vision you can help them get to. Set your needs aside temporarily.

If you want to be obsessed about something - be obsessed with their pains, circumstances, dilemmas, and personal pursuits.

Suggestions

Make a comprehensive list of all of the problems you solve or that a particular product solves for your customer. You should have 5 - 10 problems on this list.

Then, underneath each one, write down what the impact is if they don't fix it. This could be an economic impact (costs them money), a frustration impact (they're weary of dealing with it), or an internal impact (they can't advance their career).

Once you have that list, you're on your way to being able to communicate the value of your product where it matters to them. You are meeting them where they are – not thinking about your solution – but in the midst of their own problem.

How This Will Help You

1. **Increased Trust and Credibility:** By demonstrating genuine interest in understanding the customer's challenges and concerns, you will build trust and establish yourself as a credible partner who truly cares about the customer's well-being.

2. **Better Alignment with Customer Problems and Objectives:** By focusing on the customer's problems, you can tailor your recommendations to directly address the customer's specific pains, increasing the likelihood of a successful sale and long-term satisfaction. When there's no alignment, they won't see you as a solution provider or a transformational agent in their life

3. **Improved Listening Skills:** Prioritizing your customer's problems requires active listening, which will help you develop powerful communication skills. It will also help you gain insights into their motivations and decision-making process.

4. **More Effective Problem-Solving:** By understanding the customer's problems in depth, you can leverage your expertise and resources to provide awesome solutions that address their needs, positioning YOU as a valuable

partner. Positioning is key here. If you position yourself as yet another salesperson calling on them, that will not create the right atmosphere for you to get the truth.

5. **Stronger Relationships:** Adopting a customer-centric approach fosters deeper connections with customers, as they perceive you as someone who genuinely cares about their success and well-being rather than simply pushing a product or service. We are always talking about how important relationships are, but rarely do we determine what exactly builds that relationship.

6. **Differentiation from Competitors:** In a crowded marketplace, a sales professional who prioritizes understanding and solving the customer's problems can stand out from competitors who will be more focused on their own goals and agendas. As I've always said, it doesn't take much to separate you from the competition, and being focused on **their issues** is the magic key that does that.

STRATEGY 2

GET YOUR MIND RIGHT

"What we think, we become."
– Buddha

We have a saying around our training that you've heard before: "Mind Over Matter."

This means that your mind is the master key to your riches. It will influence your behavior and your results. **So get your mind right.**

One mindset you must have is that **you cannot sell to everyone.** Not everyone is a prospect for you. Once we get that into our minds, we can be judicious about who we spend time with.

If you have a good sales conversion process, you'll be able to suss out who's a good prospect and who's not. Time is the currency you trade for results. Don't waste time with non-buyers.

Suggestions

Take an area that is frustrating for you right now in your quest for higher income. Maybe your closing percentage is too low. Maybe you're not generating enough leads. **And spend some quiet time thinking about your thinking.**

Every problem we seek to resolve is first a thinking problem, then, and only then, an action problem. But no change is sustainable if you don't change the thinking behind the action.

Let's say you're uncomfortable talking about **money.** And you always leave that discussion until the end. Your thinking is that somehow money is an evil topic. You must change that.

So, as you're spending your thinking time, think about what money actually is. **It's merely the exchange of something valuable from one person to another who has something more valuable than money.**

Once you take the emotion out of money, you can talk about it at any time. We like the idea of warning people when that economics conversation is going to happen. That way, it's not a boogeyman - for you or for them.

Do you see how the change of thinking makes the money conversation easier to have?

How This Will Help You

1. **Increased Self-Awareness:** By developing the ability to evaluate your own thought processes critically, you will gain a deeper understanding of the motivations, beliefs, and biases that you have. Some of these you might be blind to without a heightened self-awareness. By doing this, you can overcome limiting mindsets, allowing you to approach

2. **Improved Decision-Making:** Our thoughts shape our decisions, and by becoming more mindful of our thought patterns, you can make more informed and strategic decisions. This can lead to better prioritization, more effective time management, and the ability to identify and pursue the most promising sales opportunities.

Think about how many decisions you make every day in your business. Anything you can do to help those decisions become more resourceful for you in the long run will help.

3. **Enhanced Emotional Intelligence:** Changing one's thinking often involves recognizing and managing emotions effectively. By developing stronger emotional intelligence, you can better navigate challenging situations, build stronger relationships with clients, and communicate more persuasively. Shining the light on any blind spots you have will help you become a rockstar.

4. **Greater Resilience:** Sales environments are constantly evolving, and the ability to adapt and bounce back from setbacks is crucial. By cultivating a growth mindset and learning to re-frame negative thoughts, sales professionals can develop greater resilience and adapt more readily to changing circumstances.

5. **Increased Confidence and Motivation:** Negative thought patterns can undermine confidence and motivation, hampering sales performance. By becoming better at challenging your own limiting beliefs and cultivating a more empowering mindset, you will experience a boost in self-confidence and motivation – which will drive you to take more proactive actions and achieve better results.

STRATEGY 3

BECOME DETACHED FROM ALL OUTCOMES

"Work hard, be kind, and amazing things will happen. Amazing things have a remarkable way of happening to those who work hard and remain kind, calm, and detached amid life's inevitable abrasions."
- Charlie Munger

The more detached you are from the outcomes in your business, the freer you will be to say what needs to be said and do what needs to be done.

Detachment is the notion that you will be fully engaged in the sales process, with your questions, with your offer, and with insights you can provide your prospect.

But at the end of the line, you must be detached from whether the customer does business with you or not. You are not entangled in the outcome. The outcome is the outcome. Detachment is the key to freedom. Just think about what will be possible if you are detached from any and all outcomes. Everything gets easier.

Suggestion

Verbalize your detachment to the deal upfront. Say something like, *"I'm really looking forward to understanding your dilemmas and any problems that you want to solve. And I'm also looking forward to sharing with you how we help our customers. But at any time during this process, if you feel like my solution is not appropriate, or I believe that your problems are not congruent with my solutions, let's have an agreement that we can end it at any time."*

How this Will Help You

1. **Reduced Stress and Anxiety:** When you are detached from outcomes, you can approach sales conversations and negotiations with a greater sense of calm and

confidence. This reduced stress and anxiety will lead to clearer thinking, better decision-making, and more effective communication. Being stressed about whether you're going to get a deal or not will not help you get the deal that you're stressed about not getting :-)

2. **Increased Authenticity and Credibility:** Detachment from outcomes allows you to be more genuine and authentic in your interactions with clients. You can focus on truly understanding the client's needs and providing valuable insights without being driven by the desperation to close a deal at any cost. This authenticity will enhance your credibility and build trust with clients.

3. **Improved Personal Income #1:** Paradoxically, by letting go of the attachment to specific outcomes, you will become more effective in your sales efforts. This increased effectiveness can lead to more closed deals and, consequently, higher personal income. When you are not clouded by the fear of failure or the pressure to meet short-term goals, you can approach each opportunity with a clear and focused mindset, which will translate into higher income.

4. **Greater Resilience and Adaptability:** Detachment from outcomes can help you bounce back more quickly from setbacks. Instead of dwelling on disappointments, you can objectively analyze the situation, learn from it, and move on to the next opportunity with renewed energy and focus. We live in a world of constant change, chaos, and market drama, so your ability to be resilient is critical in growing your business.

5. **Improved Personal Income #2:** Detachment from outcomes will also contribute to personal income growth by enabling you to take calculated risks – and explore new opportunities without being paralyzed by the fear of failure. When you are not overly attached to specific outcomes, you can be more open to experimenting with new strategies, exploring untapped markets, or pursuing ambitious goals that could potentially yield significant rewards.

STRATEGY 4

CREATE A WRITTEN STRATEGY

We rely on corporate strategy to grow a business (although most businesses fail here) so why wouldn't it be useful for you to have your own plan?

You must have a strategy that gets you from where you are to where you want to be. And that strategy should not be a 37-page business plan. That's useless.

Ask the average salesperson to share their strategy and watch what they give you. When there is no strategy, there is less intention. And intention is a 'currency' that you use to get you to your perfect outcomes.

Suggestion

Your strategy should contain three important components:

1. **Your assets:** I will deal with this portion in the next strategy (#5).

2. **Your 'becoming':** (who do you need to become to make the achievement of this strategy easy?)

3. **Your skills:** (the skills that a successful future requires - not the skills of the past).

A strategy is not to 'make a thousand cold calls a year.' Those are tactics.

Spend time with the 'three components' and document how you will deploy these elements of your strategy.

1 | Your Assets

I will deal with this portion in the next strategy.

2 | Your Becoming

I had a coach 15 years ago who always talked to me about who I was **becoming**. Not, "What do I need to do?" but "Who do you need to become to make your goals easy to achieve?"

Since then, I've always liked the "becoming" model. I use it with all of my corporate clients.

The task is very simple. Look at your goals that you have for the next 3 to 5 years. Then, ask yourself a question: "Who is the type of person who would realize these goals easily?"

Write down the attributes of that person. That person is you. But you have to have a starting point of what that person must become.

3 | Skills

Most sales organizations spend their time developing the skills of the past, not the present or the future. If you are to scale your business, one of the elements of the strategy/plan is to identify the required skill sets for your future.

So, what skills are required? Start the list. Here are a few to prompt you:

- Video skills

- Audio skills
- Interview skills
- Financial analysis skills
- Problem finding skills
- Presentation skills

Obviously, you could fill a whole page of these. But if you want to grow into your future self, your skills must be updated at all times. As a coach, it bewilders me how few salespeople have done the work here. But that's not you. I know you'll do it.

How This Will Help You

1. **Clarity of Purpose and Direction:** A written sales strategy forces you to clearly articulate your goals, target markets, unique selling propositions, and the specific actions you need to take to achieve your objectives. This clarity of purpose and direction can help you stay focused and avoid getting sidetracked by distractions or opportunities that may not align with your overall strategy.

2. **Increased Accountability and Motivation:** Having a written strategy serves as a tangible reminder of the commitments and targets you have set for yourself. This sense of accountability can act as a powerful motivator, encouraging you to take consistent action and follow

through on your plans, ultimately leading to better results. When you create a written strategy, you will be ahead of 95% of the sales professionals on this planet. Very few do this. Do it and watch how your confidence changes.

3. **Improved Time Management and Prioritization**: A well-defined strategy helps sales professionals prioritize their activities and allocate their time more effectively. By identifying the most important tasks and objectives, you will focus your efforts on high-impact activities that drive results rather than getting bogged down in less productive endeavors. As we said earlier, every day comes with a multitude of decisions you must make about where you spend your time. With a proper strategy, those decisions become easier.

STRATEGY 5

GET CLEAR ON YOUR TRUE ASSETS

"What keeps you from achieving your true potential is the under-maximization of your true assets."
- Bill Caskey

Everyone says they want more. And **more** usually means something closer to their true potential. More income. More customers. More fun. More joy.

Yet the most common mistake people make is they don't take inventory of the assets they already have. Not talking about real estate here. I'm talking about the **personal assets** that, if you brought them to bear in the marketplace, could yield fruit for years.

It's a more modern way to look at selling and achievement. Forget about closing moves and probing skills. If you wish to achieve at a level closer to your true potential – **deploy your assets better.**

Suggestion

The most commonly overlooked asset is your **knowledge base.**

If you've been in your profession for over a year, you have accumulated knowledge and wisdom about your business. Are you using that knowledge – or keeping it a secret?

Think about your results if you actually shared that knowledge with your audience. Write down **five pieces of wisdom** that you've accumulated about the business – the problems prospects have – the frameworks you've created to deliver solutions to those problems – and get to work sharing those.

You can do it in writing - in video - in audio - in webinars, or any number of other platforms.

An Example

Let's suppose you've assembled a framework of HOW you go about identifying customer problems/dilemmas. Maybe it has four steps to it. Go to canva.com and create a simple graphic that outlines those four steps. Then, in the next video you shoot, cut that graphic in as you're talking about how you go about identifying customer issues.

Your framework for how you solve problems is an asset. Think of it that way.

How This Will Help You

1. **Differentiation in a Crowded Market:** By leveraging your unique personal assets, such as specialized knowledge, life experiences, or personal traits, you can differentiate yourself from competitors and stand out in a crowded marketplace. This differentiation can make you more attractive to potential clients and increase your chances of closing deals.

2. **Stronger Relationships:** Personal assets like empathy, active listening skills, and the ability to connect with others on a deeper level can help you build stronger, more meaningful relationships with your clients. These strong connections can foster trust, loyalty, and repeat business, ultimately contributing to long-term success.

3. **Increased Personal Income:** When you effectively use your personal assets, you can become more effective in your sales approach, better understand your client's

needs, and tailor your solutions more effectively. This can lead to higher conversion rates and, ultimately, higher personal income. Why? You are better equipped to meet the demands of the market.

4. **Creation of Personal Wealth:** By fully capitalizing your personal assets, you will unlock new opportunities for growth and wealth creation. For example, leveraging your expertise and reputation could open doors to consulting opportunities, speaking engagements, or even the development of your own products or services, all of which can contribute to the accumulation of personal wealth over time.

5. **Enhanced Confidence:** Recognizing and embracing your personal assets can boost your confidence and self-esteem as you become aware of the unique strengths and value you bring to the table. This increased confidence can help you overcome obstacles, bounce back from setbacks, and persist in the face of challenges, ultimately contributing to your overall resilience and long-term success.

STRATEGY 6

CONTROL THE BUYER/SELLER DANCE

"As the guide that helps you get your prospect from where they are to where they want to be, you MUST have them sell you."
- Bill Caskey

This might be the most difficult. If you sincerely believe that you have a **premium solution** that is worth 5-10X more than the customer will pay for it, then you must work on re-creating the buyer/seller dynamic.

By that, I mean y**ou must instill in your mind the thought that the customer must convince you that they have a problem worth solving** - and that NOT solving it is NOT an option.

Honestly, this goes against everything you've probably learned in sales.

You've learned sales was a profession that requires convincing and persuasion of your prospect. I don't see it that way. The prospect has problems. You have solutions.

So why should you bear the burden of convincing them that they need to solve their own problems?

That should be on them.

If you do this correctly, they will tell you what their problems are, where they hope to get to as a result of solving them and ask you for your help.

Suggestions:

The best way to make this happen is to change the upfront dialogue you have with your potential customers; instead of going in in the "convince and persuade" mode, go in from a place of curiosity.

Say to the prospect upfront, *"I'm not really sure that my solution is perfect for you and won't know until I know a little bit more about your situation and what you're trying to accomplish. So is it OK if we spend a little time upfront talking about that, and then I can tell you whether or not we can help?"*

How This Will Help You

1. **Increased Prospect Engagement and Commitment:** When prospects actively convince themselves of the importance of solving their problems, they become more engaged and committed to the process. This heightened engagement can lead to a deeper understanding of your value and a stronger desire to find a suitable solution, increasing the likelihood of a sale.

2. **Better Alignment of Expectations:** By allowing prospects to articulate their problems, challenges, and desired outcomes, you can better align your proposed solutions with the prospects' specific needs and expectations. This alignment can result in higher customer satisfaction and a lower risk of misunderstandings or unrealistic expectations. Once you create an atmosphere where they are open to being honest with you about their issues, everything in the sales process changes. Most people can't do that. But you're reading this, so you'll be able to.

3. **Enhanced Trust:** When you create an environment that encourages prospects to sell themselves on the

need for a solution, you position yourself as a more trusted advisor rather than a pushy salesperson. This approach can foster a sense of trust and credibility, as prospects perceive the sales professional as someone who genuinely wants to help them achieve their goals rather than someone solely focused on making a sale.

4. **Improved Qualification:** By encouraging prospects to articulate their problems and convince themselves of the need for a solution, you can better qualify leads and prioritize them. This approach can help you identify prospects who are **truly** motivated to solve their problems, and then you can allocate your time and resources more effectively. Get this right, and it's a massive time saver for you.

5. **Increased Ownership and Buy-In**: When prospects take an active role in convincing themselves of the need for a solution, they develop a sense of ownership and personal investment in the process. This increased buy-in will lead to smoother implementation, better adoption of the solution, and potentially higher customer retention.

STRATEGY 7

RELY ON SYSTEMS - NOT GOALS

"It's not about having a great idea. It's about implementing it well. As with any system, process matters."
- James Clear

To properly scale your income, whether it's to the million-dollar level or something less, there are two vital ingredients: 1) A **system** that generates leads and opportunities. And 2) a **system** that takes those opportunities and converts them to clients/customers.

Very few sales professionals have a system for that. They usually rely on cold outreach and grinding out cold calls. That is not a system that scales.

Goals are great. No question about it. But systems are better. Create a system for lead generation and lead conversion, and you will never miss quota.

Suggestion - Lead Generation

The best kind of system you can build is a system where prospects call you to book appointments. Does that sound like a stretch? Maybe. But super successful companies have figured out a way to create **lead gen systems.** So should you.

It's the lifeblood of your future. Imagine waking up on Monday morning with a week of appointments with new prospects in your calendar. More in the Chapter on "Sell The Way People Buy."

Suggestion - Lead Conversion

The fact is that once a lead comes in or once a prospect expresses some interest, you need a **conversion** process that helps them go from lead to customer.

We like the idea of diagramming your conversion process. Step one. Step two. Step three. Step four. We suggest having no more than 4 to 5 steps in it.

Step 1 is typically some sort of **Discovery** step, where you and the prospect begin to understand each other and decide together whether the process is worth exploring together.

Step 2 is likely some sort of a **Deeper Peak** into their business. Maybe it's an analysis or an audit, or maybe it's talking with other people inside their company about their perspective on the issues.

Step 3 is probably a **Recommendation** of some sort.

Again, if you're in a long and complex sales cycle, you might have more sub-steps underneath each of the core. But the bottom line is you diagram, commit to a graphic, and share it with them during the first meeting. They need to know that you have a map of where you're taking them. No map – no follows.

How This Will Help You

1. **Consistency and Predictability:** Well-defined systems introduce consistency and predictability into the sales process. By following a systematic approach to lead generation, nurturing, and conversion, you can establish a reliable flow of opportunities and forecast your pipeline more accurately, reducing the uncertainty associated with ad-hoc or reactive sales strategies.

2. **Scalability:** Effective systems are designed to be scalable, allowing you to accommodate increasing demand without compromising quality. By streamlining processes and automating repetitive tasks, systems enable sales professionals to handle a larger volume of leads and prospects, facilitating sustainable growth and increased revenue potential.

3. **Improved Time Management and Productivity:** With systems in place, you can optimize your time and effort, focusing on high-value activities that drive results. By delegating or automating routine tasks, you can dedicate more time to building relationships, delivering value-added consultations, and closing deals, ultimately boosting your overall productivity and effectiveness. Ask yourself if you have systems right now that generate opportunities and convert those opportunities into sales.

STRATEGY 8

SELL THE WAY PEOPLE BUY

"The biggest problem we face as marketers is we ignore human nature. You can't fool human nature."
- Bill Caskey

Amateur sellers rely on old strategies that don't work and then, when faced with poor results, they double down on what doesn't work. They make MORE cold calls, which didn't work in the first place - and all of this ends up burning you out.

The worst part? A competitor 'across town' is using modern digital strategies to capture market share. And you don't see it. It's time to use our knowledge of human nature and modern sales strategies to build your funnel.

The fact is that people don't trust a marketer when that marketer says, "You can triple your business in three easy steps." Their BS Detector screams.

Buyers are more interested in solving current problems, so anything to help them do that will build your personal brand and lead flow.

The truth is you will get a buyer's attention if you appeal to the psychology of **problems first** and possibilities second.

Suggestions

Have a **device** that works for you in the marketplace when you are doing other things. That device could be a webinar or online event, a downloadable PDF or short booklet, a white paper, an email series that prompts people to reach out to you, or, for the advanced - a podcast or YouTube channel.

Regardless of what it is, you need something that is **always** working for you and bringing you new opportunities. Get into the 21st Century. Old thinking doesn't lead to new results.

And what do you populate that channel with? Help solve customer problems - first, by helping them identify what those problems are.

An Idea

Think about the most common mistakes your audience makes when considering the purchase of a product similar to yours. Outline these mistakes, and create a paragraph of solutions so they can avoid that mistake.

Then, offer that on your website or your LinkedIn site for people who give you their name and email address. EG. If you're in the leadership development space, and you coach leaders on how to create better environments for team productivity, your piece might be called, "7 Mistakes CEOs Make When Motivating Their Teams."

That speaks directly to their current problem. They feel helpless in trying to inspire and motivate their team to take different actions and get better results. So, your device would help them shed new light on this problem.

Plussing

Then, take each of those seven mistakes and create a video for it. In that video, share the mistake, why they make it, and what they can do to avoid it in the future.

Then, as you're shooting your video, have the document in front of you and say, "If you want to get all seven of these, direct message me below, and I will make sure you get a copy."

Don't wait for your marketing department to do this. Your marketing people will put all sorts of weird jargon in there. You're the sales professional. You're in the field every day. You speak with your prospects, and you know exactly what they're struggling with.

So there's nobody more qualified to do this than you.

How This Will Help You

1. **Increased Relevance:** By focusing on the specific problems and pains your prospects are experiencing, your lead generation efforts become highly relevant and resonate more deeply with your target audience. This relevance captures their attention and establishes an immediate connection, as prospects recognize that you understand their challenges and are well-positioned to provide valuable solutions.

2. **Enhanced Credibility and Trust:** When your lead generation content and messaging demonstrate a deep understanding of your prospects' current problems, it helps establish your credibility as an authority in your field.

Prospects are more likely to perceive you as a knowledgeable partner who can genuinely help them overcome challenges.

3. **Improved Lead Quality and Conversion Rates:** By directly addressing the problems that matter most to your prospects, your lead efforts attract prospects who are actively seeking solutions and are more likely to be engaged and motivated to take action. This targeted approach filters out less qualified leads and ensures that the leads you generate are highly relevant and more likely to convert into paying customers, optimizing your time.

STRATEGY 9

TAKE CONTROL EARLY

*"You are the **Guide**. Therefore, you should control the sales process."*
- Bill Caskey

I want you to control the sales process. Nobody else. Just you. If your mindset is that the customer controls it because they have the money that you want, you are already out of control. That's not good. If you want to scale your income, you must control the process – not the people in the process – but the process itself.

The first meeting on the phone, in person, or virtually determines your position throughout the sales process. The more needy, hungry, and attached you are in that first meeting, the more they will discount both you and your value.

Amateurs wing the first meeting.

Pros plan it out. And they plan it so they **position themselves** properly throughout.

First Meeting Suggestions:

1. Acknowledge your audience for setting aside time to see you. People love to be acknowledged.
2. Set the upfront agreement where you share with them how you'd like the meeting to go. ("Is it OK if I ask you some questions, then tell you how I work, and we can decide the next steps, if any.")
3. Ask them what they would like to accomplish as a result of this meeting.
4. Go through your questions. Have these questions planned out. Write them down so you don't forget.
5. At the end, have a clear future of what's next. ("Based on where we are, I suggest we meet again next week - what do you think?")

You don't control the process by arm-wrestling over it. You control the process by laying out the steps that you would like to take, get their buy-in on it, and proceed.

Controlling the process early is easy. You just need the right system.

How This Will Help You

1. **Establish Authority:** By taking control of the sales process from the outset, you can position yourself as a knowledgeable authority in your field. This perceived expertise and confidence can enhance your credibility in the eyes of prospects, increasing the likelihood of being taken seriously and ultimately closing deals.

2. **Shape the Narrative:** When you take charge of the sales process, you have the opportunity to shape the narrative and set realistic expectations from the beginning. This allows you to guide the conversation, address potential objections proactively, and ensure that both parties are aligned on the goals, timeline, and next steps. In our training, we talk about you being the "guide" to help your prospect get from where they are to where they want to be. Taking control early helps you help them.

3. **Maintain Efficiency:** By controlling the sales process, you keep the interactions focused and efficient. You can steer the conversation toward the most relevant topics, avoid unnecessary digressions, and ensure that valuable time and resources **are not wasted** on unproductive

discussions. Yes, your goal is to help them identify and solve problems. But your time is as valuable as theirs. Don't waste time with people who are **unwilling to allow you to guide them**.

4. **Increase Confidence/Negotiation Power:** Taking control of the sales process can boost your confidence. You will feel empowered and in command of the situation. This heightened confidence can translate into stronger negotiation skills, enabling you to secure better terms and conditions that are favorable to your interests.

5. **Enhance Prospect Experience:** When you take charge of the process, you can create a more structured and organized experience for your prospect. This minimizes confusion, reduces frustration, and leads to a more satisfying buying experience for the prospect. There is a lot written about customer experience, but we believe **prospect experience** is more important. You never have a chance to give a customer a good experience if you can't convert them from suspect to prospect to customer.

CONCLUSION

Well, I hope you've derived a great deal of value from these nine strategies. What I didn't tell you during the book is how to put these together into a training program for yourself. Because you can.

I would recommend you take the top three that appeal to you the most. and over the next 30 days, work on those three.

Now, what do I mean by "work on"?

Here's a simple way to do it: Document the three you want to work on and pop them into your phone home screen. Then, as you're planning your day, decide which one of these you will focus on that day.

Don't try to focus on all three. You have the whole month for that.

Pick one and focus on that for the day.

For you social creatures, share it with one of your colleagues. Tell them to buy the book, of course :-) and then work on these together. It always helps to have an accountability buddy.

And I would love to hear from you. Email me at info@caskeytraining.com — let me know your progress!

WHAT'S NEXT?

No this is not a pitch for you to pay me money to coach you or your people. I know that when I finish a book that I really like, I'm always interested in what could be next.

There are several ways that we can continue our journey together. Here they are:

Team Training

I have corporate clients who asked me to come in and work with their entire team for a period of time, typically a minimum of 6 months. These companies are in the B2B space, they have 5 to 25 salespeople, they have a significant financial upside, and they are willing to devote two to three hours a month to training.

There are many different ways to slice this, but typically, it's two group sessions per month and access to me for one-to-one calls. www.billcaskey.com to contact me.

1:1 Coaching

This offer is primarily for higher-income people, probably people who are earning 200k or more. I run a one-to-one coaching engagement for a minimum of 6 months. this is not inexpensive, so you need to be of a certain income level and have high upside potential. www.billcaskey.com to contact me.

Challenge Training

Each month for the foreseeable future, we will run a 5-day training series called The Million Dollar Seller Challenge. This is for individual performers who want to take this material and more like it, and implement it in their business. Many sales professionals and leaders are stuck today, not knowing how to adopt modern selling and marketing strategies to generate more revenue. And that is what this does.
www.milliondollarsellerchallenge.com